For Alexander,
the world's cleverest
Ringnecked Parakeet

Front endpapers:
photo by Harry V. Lacey

Back endpapers:
photo courtesy of Vogelpark Walsrode

A Beginner's Guide to
PARROTS

Written by
Marshall Naigh

Contents

© 1986 by T.F.H. Publications, Inc. Distributed in the UNITED STATES by T.F.H. Publications, Inc., 211 West Sylvania Avenue, Neptune City, NJ 07753; in CANADA by H & L Pet Supplies Inc., 27 Kingston Crescent, Kitchener, Ontario N2B 2T6; Rolf C. Hagen Ltd., 3225 Sartelon Street, Montreal 382 Quebec; in Canada to the Book Trade by Macmillan of Canada (A Division of Canada Publishing Corporation), 164 Commander Boulevard, Agincourt, Ontario M1S 3C7; in ENGLAND by T.F.H. Publications Limited, 4 Kier Park, Ascot, Berkshire SL5 7DS; in AUSTRALIA AND THE SOUTH PACIFIC by T.F.H. (Australia) Pty. Ltd., Box 149, Brookvale 2100 N.S.W., Australia; in NEW ZEALAND by Ross Haines & Son, Ltd., 18 Monmouth Street, Grey Lynn, Auckland 2 New Zealand; in SINGAPORE AND MALAYSIA by MPH Distributors (S) Pte., Ltd., 601 Sims Drive, #03/07/21, Singapore 1438; in the PHILIPPINES by Bio-Research, 5 Lippay Street, San Lorenzo Village, Makati Rizal; in SOUTH AFRICA by Multipet Pty. Ltd., 30 Turners Avenue, Durban 4001. Published by T.F.H. Publications, Inc. Manufactured in the United States of America by T.F.H. Publications, Inc.

1.
Introduction

Let us first welcome you to the ever growing number of people who have become interested in and have acquired a bird of the parrot family recently.

Mealy Amazon, Amazona farinosa inornata. *Photo by Earl Grossman.*

Not only are they colorfully plumaged but they lend themselves so easily to taming. In a very short time parrots can learn to sit on your finger, climb on your shoulder, pull a toy cart and talk to you.

Of course, a pet that can talk—in itself—is a most wonderful reward. With a little patience, first taming your parrot, then teaching him to talk and do tricks, you will agree wholeheartedly that a parrot is indeed a fine pet.

Parrot lore

No one can say how long parrots have been kept as pets, since their association with man goes back before the time of recorded history. As pets, it is likely they are as ancient as domestic cats and dogs. Strong evidence for the great antiquity of parrots in captivity is found by anyone who has visited primitive people throughout the tropical world. Primitive Indians of South America will tell you that they have always caught and tamed parrots. The same story is told by natives in Africa, Australia and Asia. As long as the human species has been intelligent enough to crave the companionship of animals, man has been keeping company with parrots.

The droll behavior of parrots is one of the main reasons for their popularity. The Sulphur-crested Cockatoo, Cacatua galerita, *is one of the most familiar cockatoo species. Photo by Dr. Herbert R. Axelrod.*

*The longer tailed members of the parrot family are usually called "parakeets."
This is a male Red-rumped Parakeet*, Psephotus haematonotus. *Photo by
Harry V. Lacey.*

2.
Varieties

Parrots all belong to the family *Psittacidae*, of which there are more than 300 species occurring in nearly all of the world's tropical and semi-tropical belt. They are generally very active, gregarious, strong-flying birds. To

Blue and Gold Macaw, Ara ararauna. *Photo by A. J. Mobbs.*

those who have seen them only in cages or chained to perches, this will come as a surprise. But anyone who has travelled in tropical rain forests knows them for their raucous chattering in tall trees and for their strong, erratic flight.

Parrots have distinctive features that make them easily recognizable. They have large heads and powerful curved beaks, the upper portion extending down over the lower. The upper portion is hinged and movable; this distinguishes parrots from hook-billed birds like the hawks and owls. The upper portion of a raptor's bill is fixed to the bony structure of the skull. The smallest parrots can bite hard enough to hurt. For this reason a strange bird should always be approached with caution. Parrot tongues are fat and rough, ideally adapted for shelling the nuts and crushing the fruits that form the bulk of their diet in the wild state.

The toes of parrots are made for grasping, and the short stocky legs are suited for climbing. The two middle toes point forward and the two outer ones extend backward. A long, sharp claw extends from each. Many parrots are brilliantly colored, with nearly every color imaginable represented in the family.

Most species have a loud, harsh call that is capable of much variation. This, combined with a high level of intelligence, gives them their remarkable ability to imitate human speech.

In nature most parrots nest in hollow trees. The abandoned hollows of woodpeckers and rodents are often used. Most parrots are faithful mates, and in many species both parents care for the eggs and young. Newly hatched parrots are usually naked and quite helpless.

Umbrella and Sulphur-crested cockatoo chicks, twenty-six to twenty-eight days old. Photo by Frank Nothaft.

13

They develop slowly, nourished on regurgitated food provided by the parents.

The larger parrots are capable of living for a long time. For this reason a young parrot is a good investment. There are plenty of authentic records of parrots living for thirty and even fifty years.

Small parrots and parrot-like birds

Because of their compactness, many of the smaller parrots have gained great popularity as house pets.

The main group of the little parrot, genus *Brotogeris*, is the attractive Bee Bee parrot. They are found throughout almost all the Latin American countries and are indeed friendly, dainty and diminutive copies of the larger birds, and seldom are more than about six to eight inches in length. While there are many sub species of these birds, the most popular is the Canary Winged Bee Bee. It is distinguished by its overall bright green coloring with canary yellow wing feathers in the larger section of the wing.

Sometimes these Bee Bees are advertised as "Parrotlets" although the true South American Parrotlets are even smaller. They enjoy a large sale because they are so extremely friendly and easy to tame.

Medium size parrots—Conures

Probably the most popular of these is the Half Moon of which, once again, there are many species bearing a strong resemblance not only to the larger parrots but also to the Macaws to which they are closely related. Their coloring is truly exquisite; you will find shades of

The Canary Winged Bee Bee, Brotogeris versicolorus chiriri, *is favored for its tameness and companionability. Photo by Fred Harris.*

gray, white, red and orange mixed with their basic green, depending of what part of the Latin American countries in which they are raised. They run in length approximately twelve and a half inches, and, like the Bee Bee, thrive on friendship and companionship. They tame very quickly and in no time you can expect your particular species of Conure to be clamoring to be let out of his cage, sit on your hand and shoulder, pull toys and imitate sounds.

Nanday Conure

Quite similar in type and size are the Jenday and Nanday Conures, although the Jenday with its golden head, throat and chest is more colorful.

The Nanday presents a little darker appearance than the Half Moon but is nevertheless most attractive with its overall coloring of green fringed with black and red.

An outstanding feature of its coloration is its black bill and head and there is an area of bright red immediately above the black of its legs.

Another desirable feature of the Nanday Conure is that it almost tames itself so do not be surprised to have this popular bird perching on your finger in only a few days.

In the opinion of many, the Sun (Aratinga solstitialis) *is one of the most beautiful and brilliantly colored conures. These three-year-olds are a breeding pair. Photo by Fred Harris.*

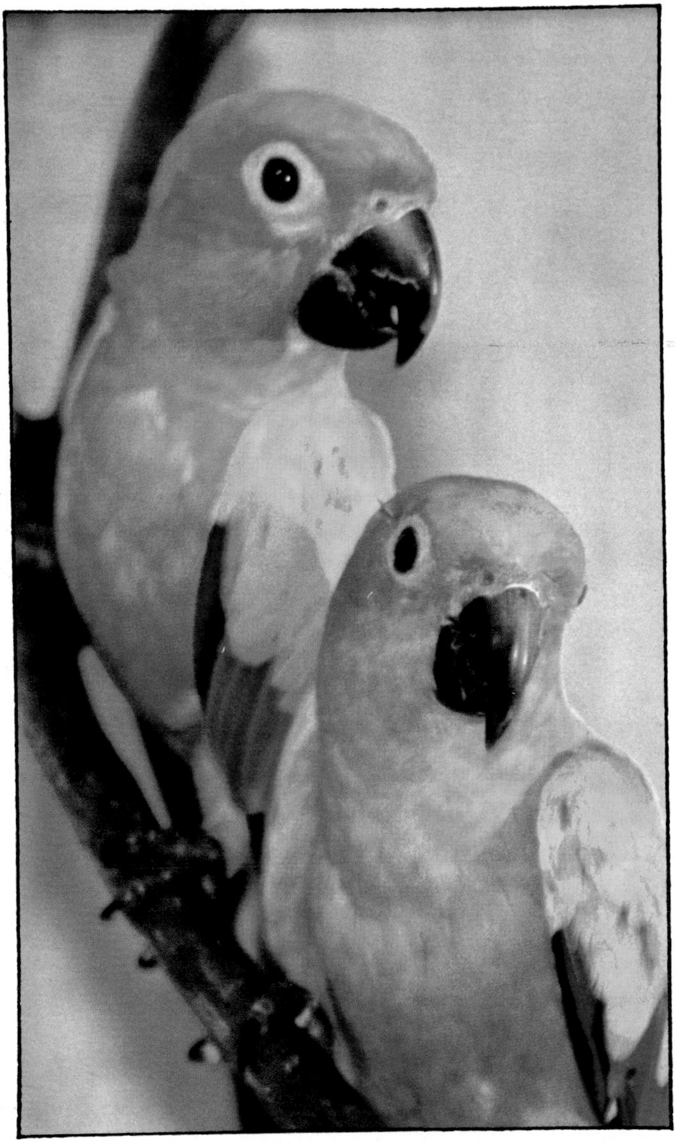

Quaker

The Quaker (actually a Parakeet), *Myiopsitta monachus*, is about the same size as the Nanday Conure. Actually, it has many of the attributes of the Nanday but its coloring is different. The overall color is green with a gray upper breast and lower head. Also most attractive in the Quaker are its deep blue larger flight feathers.

There should be no difficulty in taming the Quaker and we are certain it will be a most rewarding pet.

The larger parrots—Amazons

Everyone who has ever visited the aviary of a zoo will remember the brilliantly and different colored larger size parrots of the genus *Amazona* of which there are over 25 species distributed throughtout all the Latin countries of the Western Hemisphere. Most become extremely good talkers and appealing pets.

It would be wise at this time to call your attention to those Amazons you are most likely to see on sale in pet shops. Among the most popular are the Single and Double Yellow Head Amazons. Depending on which South American country it comes from, when first feathered the coloring on top of the head ranges from gray to blue to a light yellow. As they grow older, however, the top of the head takes on a very distinct yellow coloring.

Of the the parrots kept as pets, lovebirds, like this hand-tame Black-mask Lovebird, Agapornis personata, *are among the smallest. Photo by Vincent Serbin.*

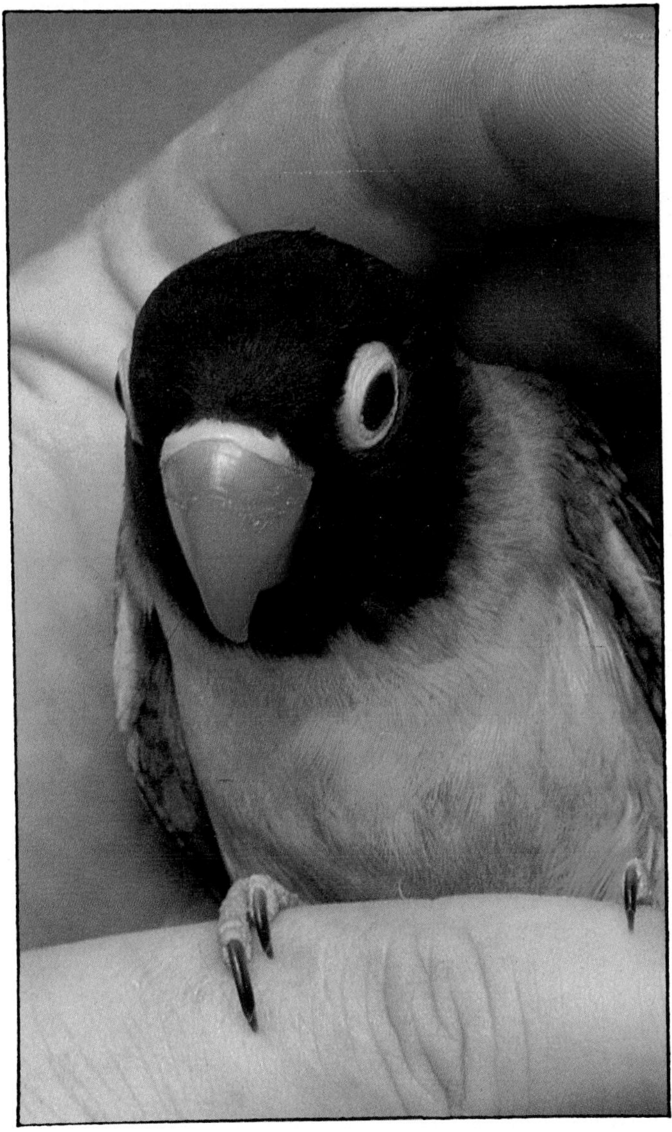

As with other species of these Amazons, there are slight variations in additional touches of red, orange and yellow throughout the overall green coloring of the bird. These little differences vary according to its country of origin.

Much the same can be said for the Double Yellow Head except that the yellow spreads more extensively over the head and comes right down to the neck of the bird, as it matures.

Oranged-winged Amazon

This is another popular Latin American species featured by a prominence of the orange coloring in its wings. Still another popular species you will find in pet stores is the Mexican Red Crown Amazon. The red gets deeper as the bird gets older thus making for a most attractive and colorful bird after a time.

Panama Amazon and Yellow Naped

These two species are frequently mistaken for each other but they are both extremely excellent talkers. Both birds have a touch of yellow on the forehead, touches of red and green on the wing and the tail. The Yellow Naped Amazon presents a much darker green appearance than the Panama species, but both are considered excellent talking pets of the Amazon family. The bill of the Panama is uniformly dark, while that of the Yellow Naped is lighter at the base.

The Spectacled Amazon

While the average Amazon runs up to about fifteen inches in length the Spectacled Amazon resembles in

A head study of the Half Moon Conure, Aratinga canicularis clarae, *which is also known as the Orange-fronted Conure. Photo by Dr. Herbert R. Axelrod.*

size that of the Conures since it is only ten to twelve inches in length, but it is stockier.

While common in certain parts of Latin America it is most frequently found in Mexico. It is quite an attractive bird since its head is crowned by almost all the prominent colors of the rainbow. This means the green overall coloring is mixed with such other colors as blue, red, yellow and white with many of these colors outlined in black feathers.

Blue Fronted or Blue Crowned Amazon

The Blue Fronted Amazon is considered one of the most desirable species and is famous for its ability to talk. Its name "Blue Fronted" probably comes from the definite blue on the forehead mixed with some yellow as the bird gets older.

Its native habitat is principally the tropical countries of South America. It has other touches of red, green, even black, varying from its particular area of origin.

Mealy Amazon

Although this species of Amazon is mostly all green the Mealy also ranks with the best of the Amazon talkers. It is of good size and proportions and many aviarists favor it for its ability to talk even over more colorful species of the Amazon family which might be more attractive in coloring.

There are, of course, many other types of Amazon parrots through out the Latin countries of the Western Continent. We believe, however, the aforementioned species are the species you are most likely to see in pet stores.

The Double Yellow Head Amazon, Amazona oratrix. *Photo by Dr. E. J. Mulawka.*

African Grey Parrot *(Psittacus erithacus erithacus)*

It is the consensus of parrot specialists that the African Grey of all parrot and parrot-like birds is probably the best talker. It is admired not only for its ability to learn many different words but aviarists agree that the words of the African Grey resemble human speech more than any other.

True, it is one of the most expensive of the parrot-type birds but this comes not only from its ability to talk but because of its own distinctive coloring.

As its name would imply, the overall color is a shiny gray mixed with touches of black. Worked into this pattern are touches of red and white. The tail is bright red. The African Grey tames quite readily and almost immediately begins to mimic voices and sounds.

Larger and/or exotic birds

The Macaw is probably the largest member of the parrot family. While an exact account might be difficult to make, there are about 25 known species of Macaw.

They are characterized by their large size, some of them running to thirty-six inches in length including the tail, with appropriately long beaks and tails. Another characteristic of the Macaw is its wide variety and range of coloring. Truly, almost every color of the rainbow could be located in one or more members of the Macaw family.

The same method used in taming and training parrots should be used for the Macaws except we caution, because of the size of the parrot, to be sure that a heavy glove is used, expecially in the preliminary training.

They, too, are natives of the Latin American countries and some of the most popular species are: Hyacinth Macaw, Lear's Macaw, Military Macaw, Blue and Gold Macaw, and Green Winged Macaw.

Lovebirds

Lovebirds from Africa were more popular years ago, but they are still desirable because they are hardy, long-lived, good breeders, and are adept at learning tricks. Lovebirds get their common name from the affection and devotion pairs of them show to each other in captivity.

Of the ten known species of Lovebirds only three and one sport are commonly sold in pet stores.

These are: the Peach-face (*Agapornis roseicollis*), the Black-mask (*Agapornis personata*), the Fischers (*Agapornis fischeri*), and the Blue-mask which is a mutant or sport of the Black-mask.

Parrotlets

These birds are the South American counterparts of the African Lovebirds, which they resemble although they are smaller and more slender. They also look like miniature Amazons, but they grow to only 5 inches.

Cockatoos

Cockatoos are extremely handsome birds native to Aus-

Probably no parrot species is more famed than the splendidly colored Scarlet Macaw, Ara macao, now an endangered species in the wild. Photo by Ray Hanson.

tralia and the islands of Australasia. They have crests on the top of the head, which they can raise or lower at will, but in some species the crest is more prominent than in others. In the farming regions of Australia cockatoos are very unpopular because large flocks of them descend upon farm fields to feed on grain.

The following species of cockatoos are occasionally brought in: Greater Sulphur-Crested *(Kakatoe galerita)*, Lesser Sulphur-Crested *(Kakatoe sulphurea)*, Lead-beater's *(Kakatoe leadbeateri)*, and the Long-Billed *(Kakatoe tenuirostris)*.

Cockatiel *(Nymphicus hollandicus)*

The Cockatiel is a smaller cousin of the cockatoo. They average about 12 inches long, and are native to Australia. Cockatiels make fine pets, and they become fair talkers although their high-pitched voices make them a little hard to understand. They also learn to whistle tunes.

Their predominant color is gray, with a yellow face and crest. In the center of the yellow patch is a large orange spot. The front edges of the wings are white. Cockatiels are plentiful and inexpensive. Females generally lack the orange spot and have barred outer tail feathers. Immature males resemble females.

3.
Selection

There are thousands of colorful, appealing birds through out the world that would make nice pets—if they could be domesticated. If you have ever attempted to keep any of our common wild birds you know that

Of the amazons, the Orange-winged, Amazona amazonica, *is one of the species most consistently available in pet shops. Photo by Dr. Herbert R. Axelrod.*

most of them just don't adapt to confinement. It is a distressing experience to watch a song bird dash itself to death in a cage or collapse and die of fright before your eyes.

This is not true of parrots: they adapt readily to captivity even when captured as adults, and they frequently develop a strong attachment to their owner. Apparently something in their well-developed brain helps them to adjust to strange conditions.

Still there are plenty of other birds that can be domesticated, but parrots possess special attributes that place them at the very top as pet birds.

Nearly everyone associates parrots with the ability to talk. This is what sets them apart from other colorful birds. Compare a parrot's head with its body and then

FACING PAGE: *By now the Cockatiel is thoroughly domesticated. All those found in pet shops are captive bred. Photo by Michael Gilroy.* BELOW: *Parrots, like these Nanday Conures,* Nandayus nenday, *tuck their heads back between their wings when sleeping. Photo by Dr. Herbert R. Axelrod.*

make a similar comparison with other birds. You will find that the parrots have very large heads for the body size. The large, well-developed brain provides them with the intelligence to imitate the human voice and to learn delightful tricks.

Patience on your part will be well rewarded in your enjoyment from your parrot. Do not rush or try to accomplish too much at one time.

Color is another important attribute of parrots. Pick a color—any color—and somewhere in the world there is a member of the parrot family sporting that color in its plumage.

Once adjusted to their owners, parrots are friendly birds. Often they develop warm devotion to their masters.

Parrots are easy to care for. Give them the warmth of an average home, pleasant surroundings, clean living quarters, the simple foods they require, and all they ask in addition is love and affection. Few pets require so little for the satisfaction and pleasure they so generously give.

It is almost like having another baby in the home. Yes, many of the joys of a child are duplicated in the ownership of a parrot. You will hear them scold for food or indicate a desire to play with you and you will almost feel a sense of gratitude when they are with or amongst your family.

4.
Care

The first consideration in the care of a parrot is kindness. No animal can be expected to become a devoted pet if it is mistreated. Parrots, especially, are quick to sense the love of an owner and they respond to it. Chil-

Because parrots as a group are chewers, the larger the species, the more sturdy the cage must be. Photo courtesy of Bird Depot, Inc.

ABOVE: *Perches of tree branches give a parrot something to gnaw on. Photo by Max Mills.* FACING PAGE: *Bryan Hinterbrandt with young hand-reared Single Yellow Head Amazons. Photo by Louise Van der Meid.*

dren (and some adults) must be instructed never to scare or tease them. Incidentally, this is an important additional reason for bringing any pet into a household: to teach children kindness. Parrots should never be punished. Although they are intelligent, they are not bright enough to know they are being punished. In days fortunately gone by, parrots being trained were often rapped on the head when they failed to respond to instructions. The result invariably was a noisy, nasty or terrified bird. In everything done to and for a parrot, kindness must be kept in mind.

Parrots are comparatively easy to care for. So long as you provide their daily food, plus perhaps a Polly treat, and fresh water daily, they will be happy and survive. Of course, the usual minimum sanitary care should be provided, the cage cleaned when required, perches or sticks scraped from time to time. Actually, many parrots like to sit on top of their cage or on some kind of perch thereon. They are also easily trained to follow you about the house and take delight in amusing antics outside of their cage. Various types of toys for parrots are available at your favorite pet store. Ladders, mirrors, balls, bells, etc. are only a few.

Cages make the most satisfactory homes in most situations. They should be large enough to allow the bird to move without difficulty. Square cages are best. The cage should be provided with two or more stout wooden perches and be changeable from the outside. The bottom of the cage should be removable for cleaning.

Cages should be constructed of metal since wooden cages are quickly chewed to pieces. The cage should be located in a bright place away from drafts. In front of windows is fine. If the location is sunny, cover part of the front of the cage to prevent overheating.

For the serious hobbyist with several parrots, an aviary is the ideal enclosure. A well-designed aviary provides parrots with room for exercise, flight, and nesting. In mild climates, the aviary may be built outdoors.

Aviaries must be of sturdy construction, since parrots are strong and active. If the aviary is outdoors it must be built to keep out the neighbor's cat and wild predators.

Whether or not breeding is desired, an aviary should have nesting boxes, with holes just large enough for entry. The number of boxes required will depend upon the number of birds in the aviary. If the box is made of wood it will eventually be chewed up. For the larger parrots such as cockatoos, many owners use small galvanized garbage pails with a hole cut in the side. For the smaller birds pet shops carry ready-made boxes. Regardless of what is used, the box should have a removable top for cleaning and observation. The nesting box should be several feet off the floor, perhaps fastened to the side of the aviary.

All parrots are adapted to tropical or sub-tropical climates. Hence, they cannot endure extreme cold. Parrots kept outdoors in the summer or in southern parts of the United States can endure fairly cold temperatures if they have lots of room to move about. However, parrots kept in small cages, indoors or out, quickly succumb when the temperature falls. If the temperature of your house drops at night, the cage should be covered. If it is necessary to take a parrot outdoors in the winter, the cage should be carefully covered and brought indoors as quickly as possible.

A spray bath is enjoyed by many pet parrots, but it seems unusual that this Grey tolerates such a drenching! Photo by Louise Van der Meid.

Cleaning

Cleanliness is said to be next to godliness. In addition to that cleanliness fortifies good health. A parrot that is kept in a dirty cage is much more likely to contract a disease then one kept in clean surroundings. Also, a parrot maintained in a clean cage is much more appealing aesthetically. Parrots enjoy taking a bath once in a while. They can be placed out in a warm summer rain or they will enjoy standing under a lukewarm shower. Pet shops also offer a variety of bird baths.

Some chores must be done daily if a parrot is to remain in the best of health. Water must be changed every day. Food should be checked periodically. If the food is fresh fruit or greens, it should not be allowed to rot. The floor of the cage must be cleaned several times a week. About once a week remove the parrot from its cage while the cage is being given a scrubbing with hot soapy water, thoroughly rinsed and dried.

Feeding equipment

Most cages come with food and water containers that can be serviced from the outside. These are best. But almost any small container can be used to hold feed. If it is fairly high, a container should have an edge that permits the bird to stand on it. Containers so large as to permit the bird to stand in them are not desirable. With a large container a parrot will scatter seed and will mix its own waste with the food. Pet shops sell a variety of feeders, one that's sure to suit your needs.

5.
Feeding

Parrot owners are indeed fortunate that commercially prepared Polly food is available at most pet stores. It provides a mixture of ingredients that are wholesome

Many pet parrots are quite content to remain on a stand, provided they have food and water available. Photo courtesy of Bird Depot, Inc.

and meet the basic requirements of a daily food for these birds.

Cuttlebone or ground oyster shell should also be provided for calcium. Many parrots will eat a wide variety of fruits which are good for them.

Bananas especially are enjoyed by parrots. Fruits should be fed sparingly at first because they may cause diarrhea until the bird's system becomes accustomed to them; the same applies to greens.

All seed-eating birds must have gravel because birds have no teeth with which to chew their food. Mixed with the hard seeds in the bird's gizzard, gravel helps to grind the seeds up. Don't use gravel from roads or driveways as it may contain tar, plant poison, insecti-

A seed mix for parrots often contains sunflower seeds and peanuts, among others. Photo by Dr. Herbert R. Axelrod.

Perch rings, mineral blocks, and cuttlebone help to satisfy a pet parrot's need to gnaw. Photo by Wayne Wallace.

cides or other harmful substances. Limestone and shells alone are unsatisfactory because they dissolve too readily. It is best to purchase gravel from the pet store, since such gravel is prepared expecially for birds. Nuts in their shells may be given as an occasional treat. Once again, a commercially prepared Polly treat is available at your favorite pet shop. You can actually help train, tame and teach your bird to do little tricks and obey your orders by giving him some of this Polly treat after he does perform successfully for you.

Another treat that parrots enjoy and one that is available at pet stores is a biscuit-like puffed treat. It will be most interesting to see your pet pick these biscuit treats up in his claws, and play with them before finally eating them with relish.

6.
Training

Without training, a parrot is of little more value to a home than a decorative vase or a colorful painting. With training, a parrot can become a never-ending source of pleasure. Thus every parrot should be tamed, at the

ABOVE: *Hand taming is the result of gaining your pet's trust. Photo by Louise Van der Meid.* FACING PAGE: *The African Grey Parrot,* Psittacus erithacus. *Photo by Max Mills.*

Lying on its back is an extremely unnatural position for a parrot—not every parrot can be expected to do so. Photo by Dr. E. J. Mulawka.

very least, to the extent of being willing to perch on one's finger. At best they can be trained to do delightful tricks and many species can be taught to imitate human words.

Before teaching your parrot to talk, best results are obtained by first taming and training your bird.

Taming a parrot takes patience and at all times an attitude of affection. The first step is to gain the parrot's confidence. Sudden movement should be avoided. For the first few days, you should frequently approach the bird slowly and talk to him in a normal voice. In that way, a parrot becomes accustomed to you. You can show affection by offering little pieces of fruit such as banana or a grape from your fingers.

The next step is to teach your pet to sit on a stick while he is still in his cage. Slowly approach the cage talking gently to the bird and open the cage door. Gently, place a perch or stick under his breast and exert a little pressure. Chances are the bird will transfer its grip from the cage perch to the stick in your hand. If he does not respond at first, keep trying, all the time talking in a gentle affectionate voice. If your bird becomes annoyed at first, stop after five or ten minutes until another time. In a short while most parrots become accustomed to stepping up on the stick in your hand. Please do not forget to wear a glove as it is possible at first the bird may nip or scratch.

Once the bird learns to perch on your stick, while he is still in the cage take another perch in your other hand. And teach your parrot to climb from the stick in one hand to the other.

When the above progress has been satisfactorily attained, but still using a glove, have your parrot grasp the stick in one hand but now, get him to step on the gloved finger of your other hand rather than another stick. This, also, should be accomplished in a short time and you can dispense with the sticks so that your parrot will readily go from the gloved finger of one hand to that of the other. At this point you are now ready to draw the parrot from the cage on your finger (in some instances if your bird refuses to leave the cage on your finger, it might be best to draw him from the cage on a perch first and then transfer him to the gloved finger of your other hand).

There have been some thoughts pro and con about having the flight feathers of a parrot cut or removed by your veterinarian. Most fanciers believe this is unneces-

Parrot training comes easiest if it capitalizes on the bird's natural movements. Photo by Dr. Herbert R. Axelrod.

sary unless you customarily keep your bird outdoors and might want to remove him from his cage in a backyard or outdoor porch. Then, perhaps, it might be best to have your veterinarian remove the flight feathers to avoid the possibility of your pet parrot flying up to high trees. It has been said that of all domesticated pets, no other pet provides the fun and enjoyment of a trained parrot, perhaps even more so than a trained dog. The patience you have displayed in properly taming and training your pet parrot will be amply rewarded by his friendship and companionship outside his cage.

The smaller parrots are trained in the same manner but often hand tame much quicker. Usually, by inserting a perch or your hand into the cage, the smaller parrots will at first remain on your hand or perch only momentarily, then jump off. However, in a surprisingly short time you will find that this smaller parrot will then remain on your hand or perch. Then, of course, it is time to start taking the bird out of the cage, following the same procedure mentioned earlier in this section.

A parrot that has become thoroughly tame may actually enjoy being handled. Some even like to be roughed up a bit, responding by gently nibbling their owner's hand.

In bird shows, trained parrots skate and ride trucks, just as this Green Winged Macaw, Ara chloroptera, *is doing. Photo by Dr. Herbert R. Axelrod.*

This Hyacinth Macaw has been taught to play dead. Photo by Dr. Herbert R. Axelrod.

Once tame, a parrot can be taught a wide variety of simple tricks much the way a dog is taught. By watching the bird's natural inclination it will be possible to get ideas for tricks that can be learned. Parrots have been taught to pull miniature wagons, to ring bells, to do somersaults, to walk on tightropes, to ride on toys and to do many other amusing things.

7.
Talking

Teaching a parrot to talk requires more patience than does handtraining, but the reward will be worth the effort. Some kinds of parrots become better talkers than others. Young birds become better talkers than mature

Parrots no doubt become tame because of a need for companionship. Photo by Dr. E. J. Mulawka.

birds. A really tame parrot will become a better talker than a partially tamed one. Hence, a thorough job of training before you attempt to teach the bird to talk is of great importance.

Women's and children's voices are more easily imitated than men's voices. Only one voice should do the training, as several different voices will be confusing. If you have a record player you can buy training records that will save you much of the effort of repeating words until the parrot learns them.

Parrots learn to talk more readily when there are no distractions. During the training session, the radio and television must be turned off, and if there are other people present, they must remain quiet. Some parrot owners remove even visual distractions by covering the cage during a training session. If, after a training period, the parrot is heard attempting to say the word being taught, the owner should repeat it promptly to aid the bird in saying it correctly.

In training a parrot to talk, it must be remembered they are intelligent as birds go, but you should keep your words or phrases very short and stick to ones with clear, distinct sounds. Keep repeating the bird's name, the names of people in your household which he will hear constantly; you will even be surprised at his ability to pick up telephone calls especially if they are repeated often.

It has been scientifically proven that a parrot CAN associate words with meaning. People are sometimes fooled into believing that a parrot can only imitate sounds; we can only say that you will often be quite surprised to hear an intelligent reply to something said either to the parrot or to somebody else in the room.

The first words are the most difficult to teach. Generally speaking, the more words a parrot learns, the more easily it learns, for it is forming the habit of imitating human speech. Once a parrot has the habit deeply ingrained, it may imitate conversation so readily that it becomes a nuisance. Keep this in mind when selecting words to be taught because you may be starting something you can't stop.

Parrot breeder Don Mathews with a young Double Yellow Head that was reared by hand. Photo courtesy of Don Mathews.

8.
Ailments

Once a parrot has become tame enough to be handled, it should periodically be removed from its cage and carefully examined. Look for injuries, unusual swellings, and ingrown feathers. Look carefully under the

ABOVE: *Ill birds, like this White-eyed Conure,* Aratinga leucophthalmus, *seldom show much evidence that they are not well. Photo by Tony Silva.* FACING PAGE: *The Yellow Nape,* Amazona auropalliata, *may be the best talker of all the amazons. Photo by Dr. Herbert R. Axelrod.*

feathers for mites and lice. Droppings if caked on feathers or legs should be washed off. If any unusual signs are noted, the bird should be taken to a veterinarian experienced with birds. (While some vets have had much experience with cage birds, there are others who know little about them.)

Even without an examination, a parrot may appear obviously ill. Some signs of sick birds: the bird sits dejectedly with its feathers fluffed out; diarrhea; irregular or noisy breathing; refusal to eat; swellings or lumps. Since parrots are temperamental birds they may show some of these symptoms for brief periods without anything serious being wrong, but if they persist, illness must be suspected.

Feather plucking

Parrots that pull out their feathers may have a skin irritation or they may be merely bored. In either case the result can be a bedraggled unsightly bird. Some birds become habitual feather-pullers; for these usually nothing can be done. The condition should be corrected before it becomes a habit. If it is caused by skin irritation, the cause may be malnutrition. Improved diet and vitamin supplements may help. Irritation can also be caused by mites or lice. This will be discussed more thoroughly later.

If boredom is the cause of feather-plucking, placing small toys and other entertaining objects in the cage may divert the bird. Some aviculturists recommend placing the bird's cage outdoors to give it a new distraction.

Foot and beak disorders

Disorders of this kind are sometimes not diseases but simple malfunctions. Beaks and toenails can grow too long. The keeper must keep them clipped. Some parrots suffer from overgrown beaks; so do parakeets. If you are hesitant about trimming them get professional assistance. Use sharp straight nail nippers made especially for birds. These nail nippers can be purchased at your local pet shop. Trimming will not hurt the bird although there may be a little blood. Before you begin trimming a beak, study a bird with a normal beak or a close-up photo of a bird's head and shape your pet's beak accordingly.

Untrimmed nails can curve back in such a way that the bird cannot grip its perch. With nail clippers or nail nippers, snip off the tips. Avoid the dark vein running down the inside of the nail; cut short of this. If there is a little bleeding, use a styptic pencil to staunch the flow of blood. The one real foot disease is called *Bumblefoot*. This is a painful swelling of the foot caused by wrong diet or lack of exercise. The swelling will have to be relieved by a veterinarian who will lance the swelling to relieve it of pus and the cheese-like secretion.

French molt

Loosely speaking, this is a catch-all term used to designate various feather ailments. Specifically it designates an unnatural condition in which a bird is constantly molting, losing old feathers, growing new ones...so at no one time does the bird appear sleek and fully feathered as it should. Sometimes, too, a false molt will be induced by too much heat or sunlight. Most birds, normally, molt twice a year—in spring and late summer—

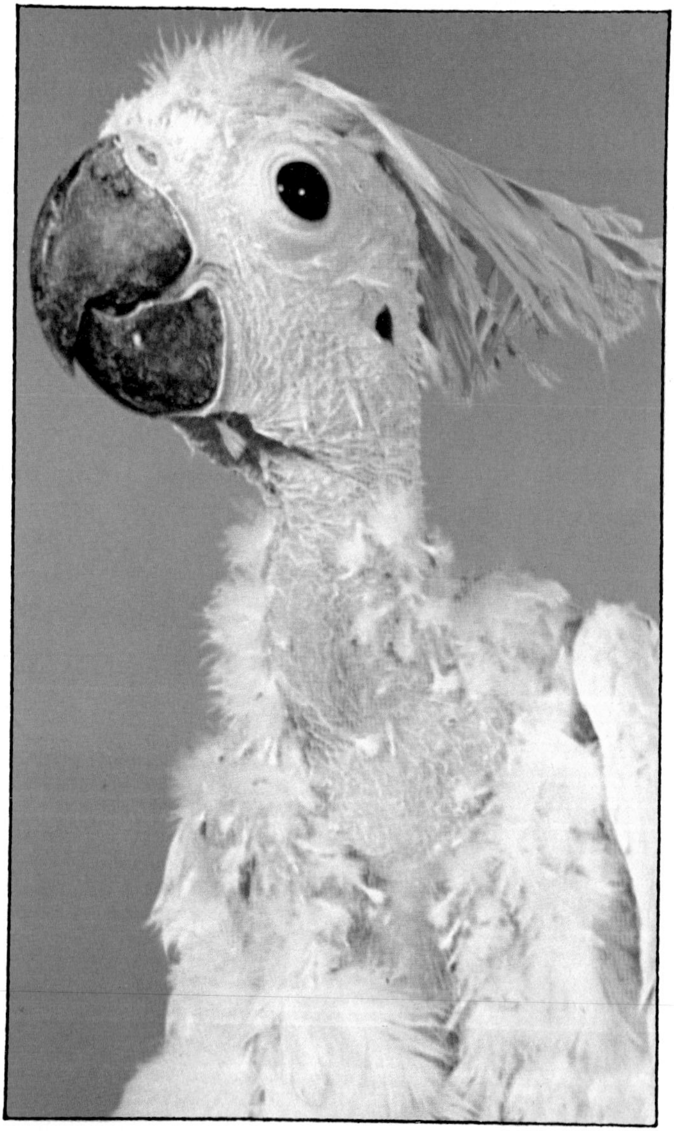

for two or three weeks each time. Parrots, however, kept indoors, molt a little constantly because of the artificial conditions. But if there is any molting that seems extraordinary, attention should be paid at once, because excessive molting can so weaken a bird that it will die.

While the causes of French Molt are uncertain, most aviarists recommend that in addition to their daily food, the birds also receive almost daily portions of the Polly treat and/or the Polly biscuit.

Move the cage of the molting bird to a cooler spot out of strong light. Make sure that it is nowhere near a radiator.

Going light

This term is widely used for a bird that is in general decline. It is not a specific ailment. The bird appears to lose substance. When picked up it seems to weigh less. If the cause is not found, the bird is likely to die.

Diarrhea and constipation

Both of these are symptoms of some other ailment. Sometimes either condition can be remedied by administering a mild laxative, which will cleanse the intestinal tract. Administering of commercially prepared products as directed will then adjust the trouble. Changes in diet can cause diarrhea. If either condition persists, the bird should be taken to a veterinarian experienced with parrots.

FACING PAGE: *In many cases it is difficult to determine why parrots pluck their own feathers, as this Citron Crested Cockatoo has. Photo by Steve Kates.*

Parasites

Individual parrots kept as house pets usually do not have mites and lice because they do not come into contact with other birds. But a newly purchased parrot may have some parasites. When mites or lice are detected, they may be treated with an insecticide spray purchased at your pet store. Since the cage may harbor mites and lice as well as the birds themselves, the cage should be thoroughly scrubbed with hot soapy water.

Broken bones

If at all possible, wrap a gauze bandage around the body to immobilize the bird and take him to the vet. If you feel competent enough to "do it yourself", follow these instructions: if the wing is broken, fold the wing into its

A bird louse on the vane of a feather. External parasites can be controlled by appropriately administered insecticides. Photo by Dr. Manfred Heidenreich.

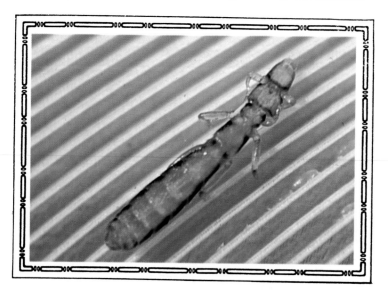

natural position with the bone ends touching and wind a one-inch strip of gauze about the body, and under the other wing, several times, holding it in place with strips of adhesive tape. Leave it on for about three weeks.

If a leg is broken, make a tiny plaster cast. Use surgeon's plaster, available in most pet stores. Have an assistant hold the leg outstretched with the bone ends touching. Apply a thin layer of plaster to the leg, and as it sets, press three half-lengths of flat toothpicks into it, and add a little more plaster. Now wind a narrow strip of gauze around the mass so that it sticks to the adhesive, and hold the bird in position until the cast sets. Allow it to remain in place for three weeks at least. At the end of that time, remove the cast carefully. Vinegar will help to dissolve the plaster.

Respiratory diseases

Parrots are subject to colds, pneumonia and clogged nasal passages. As with humans, the best treatment is rest, good diet and avoidance of chills. Antibiotics for birds, available from pet shops, should prove helpful.

In summary, prevention is the best method of combatting disease. Clean surroundings, a nutritious diet, and the sense of well-being that comes from tender loving care will go a long way towards preventing most ailments.

A general treatment, suitable in almost all cases, is the application of heat. A bird's temperature is much higher than that of a human, some being normally 109°F. With their small size their reserves of fat are limited and it is a constant struggle for them to maintain their body heat. This is why a sick bird ruffles its feathers. This action creates air pockets which act as insulation. A small bulb kept burning 24 hours a day alongside the cage makes a good additional source of heat. In extreme cases a towel can be used to cover both cage and bulb to create a heat "tent". Care must be taken to prevent the flammable cloth touching the bulb. A temperature of 85 to 90°F. maintained this way is extremely beneficial.

And don't worry about the light preventing the bird sleeping. It'll just tuck its head under its wing and will not be bothered in the least.

A towel is often an effective restraint for simple procedures like claw clipping. Photo by Dr. E. W. Burr.

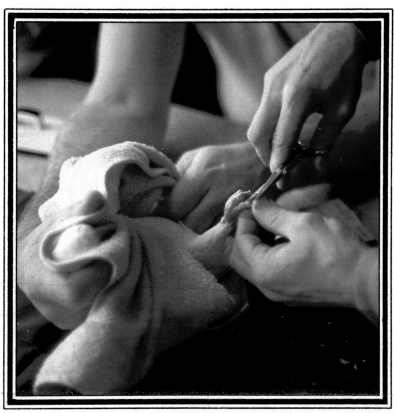

9.
Conclusion

Many more people will become parrot fanciers; many of those who now keep one parrot will be inclined to become collectors of parrots. But regardless of how many or how few a parrot fancier keeps, he must follow the

The Spectacled, or White Fronted, Amazon, Amazona albifrons. *Photo by Dr. John Moore.*

principles laid down in this book. If a fancier who now keeps one bird poorly acquires more parrots, conditions will inevitably become worse. One parrot or many, they all need to be treated with kindness and affection. The basic principles of good diet must be followed systematically. Cleanliness must be maintained. And last but far from least, every parrot should receive some training. Given the good care they deserve, parrots are the most delightful and longest lived pets in the world.

One of the larger amazon species, the Blue Front, Amazona aestiva, *is quite variable in the amount of blue and yellow it shows. Photo by Ralph Kaehler.*

Suggested Reading

PARROTS OF THE WORLD
By Joseph M. Forshaw
ISBN 0-87666-959-3
TFH PS-753

Contents: This book covers every species and subspecies of parrot in the world, including those recently extinct. Information is presented in the distribution, status, habitats and general habits. Almost 500 species and subspecies are illustrated in full color on large color plates.

Audience: This remarkable and beautiful book, valued almost as much for its sheer good looks as for its highly valuable information, is a delight to bird-lovers and book-lovers alike.

Covers lories, lorikeets, cockatoos, pygmy parrots, parrots, parakeets, macaws, cockatiels, lovebirds, hanging parrots, conures, parrotlets, caiques—every parrot in the world.

Hard cover, 584 pages, 9½ x 12½"
Almost 300 large color plates depicting close to 500 different parrots; many line illustrations.

PARROTS AND RELATED BIRDS
By Henry J. Bates and Robert L. Busenbark
ISBN 0-87666-967-4   New Edition
TFH H-912

Contents: Introduction To Parrots In Aviculture. Feeding. Aviaries And Equipment. Taming. Talking. The Caged Household Pet. Genetics And Hybridizing. Diseases. The Parrot Family. Three Unusual Subfamilies. Lories, Lorikeets And Closely Related Birds. Cockatoos. Macaws And Conures. Parrots. Parakeets. Love Birds And Parrotlets. Hanging Parrots And Guaiabero. Color Varieties Of Budgerigars. Additional Descriptions And Data On Species. Additional Data On Sex Determination, Breeding And Hand Feeding.

Audience: This is the "bible" for parrot lovers. It has more color photographs and more information on parrots than any other single book on the subject. One of the bestselling books on our list. New editions are issued regularly, with new color photographs added with each new edition. Written primarily for the owner of more than one parrot or parrot-like bird. A necessary reference work for libraries, pet shops, and airport officials who must identify imported birds.

This book is available in a new edition; more color photos are now included in the book in addition to updated nomenclature, and the structure of the book has been revised for easier reading.

Hard cover, 5½ x 8½", 494 pages
107 black and white photos, 160 color photos.

TRAINING YOUR PARROT
By Kevin P. Murphy
ISBN 0-87666-872-4
TFH H-1056

Contents: Introduction. The Pet Parrot In Your Home. Selecting Your Parrot. Housing and Equipment. Daily Care. Taming. Speech Training.

Audience: For anyone interested in making sure that he gets the most from a parrot or parrots by way of the satisfaction of owning a bird that will be a true companion instead of just an avian boarder. Loaded with good advice and full-color photos. Ages 13 and up.

Hard cover, 5½ x 8", 192 pages
72 full-color photos, 55 black and white photos, 2 line drawings.